# Hair of the Dog

DOG 'n' BONE

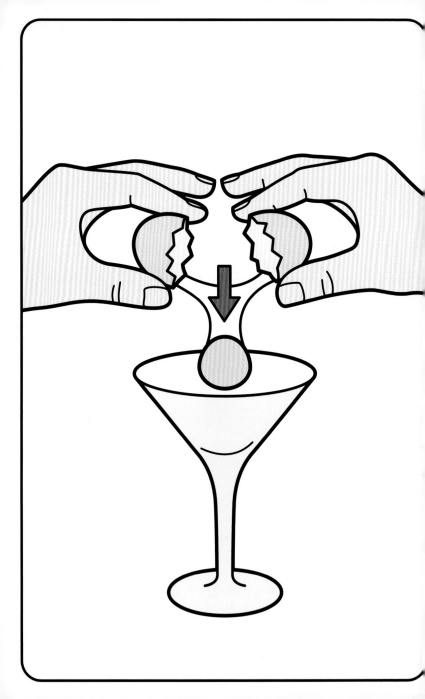

# Hair of the Dog

### and Other Hangover Cures

Dominic Bliss

DOG 'n' BONE

Published in 2012 by Dog 'n' Bone Books
An imprint of Ryland Peters & Small Ltd

20–21 Jockey's Fields          519 Broadway, 5th Floor
London WC1R 4BW                New York, NY 10012

www.dogandbonebooks.com

10 9 8 7 6 5 4 3 2 1

Text © Dominic Bliss 2012
Design and photography © Dog 'n' Bone Books 2012

A CIP catalog record for this book is available from the Library of Congress and the British Library.

ISBN: 978 0 957140 95 0

Printed in China

Editor: Pete Jorgensen
Designer: Ashley Western
Illustration: Stephen Dew

For digital editions, visit www.cicobooks.com/apps.php

# Contents

# Introduction

Here's the bad news: there's no guaranteed cure for a hangover. After a long night of seriously irresponsible boozing, it's unfortunately inevitable that you'll have at least a brief visit from Mr. Headache, Mrs. Nausea, and their unbearable kids Dizziness, Dehydration, and Stomach Upset.

However, the good news is that your house guests don't need to hang around all day. There are many different ways to ease the symptoms of excessive drinking. In this book you'll discover all sorts of remedies, ranging from alternative medicine, food recipes, and drinks (both hair of the dog and virgin) to activities, pharmaceuticals, and old wives' tales.

So what exactly happens to your body when the hangover kicks in? Alcohol contains toxins which are distributed round your body via the bloodstream. As your liver breaks down this alcohol, it creates a rather nasty substance called acetaldehyde. In small amounts, this is okay, but drink too much and it builds up in the body, causing nausea and headaches.

The headaches are made even worse by alcohol's diuretic effect. For every drink you down, you expel four times as much in urine, dehydrating you massively. As the water is drawn away from your brain, these headaches get worse because the brain shrinks, pulling on the membranes that attach it to the skull. No wonder it feels like a skunk has crawled into your head and died overnight.

All this is exacerbated by a poor night's sleep. Alcohol causes your body to produce less of the natural stimulant glutamine. Once you stop drinking, your body then goes into glutamine overdrive, making you toss and turn all night.

But enough of the science stuff. The reason you're reading this book is because you have a monumental hangover. You don't want to waste what few brain cells you have left worrying about acetaldehyde and glutamine. What you need is a remedy. Take your pick from the very best we have selected.

# The Cures

# The Water Remedy

+ lots of isotonic sports drink
+ a prison shower or ice-cold mountain lake

You need to rehydrate, and rehydrate fast. Isotonic sports drinks are best for this. They contain salts and sugars similar in concentration to those found naturally in the body.

While you're putting water back into your insides, it's a good idea to give your outsides a similar treatment. However terrible you feel the morning after, a cold shower will blow away the cobwebs. Just don't bend down for the soap. (No, really. By leaning over, the body will pump more blood to your brain and your headache will get even worse.)

Even better than a cold shower is full-body immersion. What about a dip in the ocean or an ice-cold mountain lake?

### Liquid Legends

Had Harry Potter been a boozer, he might have favored this witchcraft hangover remedy. It involves brewing tea from the shrub damiana, a plant that according to Mexican folklore was used in the original recipe for margarita cocktails. Apparently, it's also an aphrodisiac. Watch out, Hermione!

# The Sauna

+ a sauna
+ lots of drinking water
+ twigs and snow (optional)

When it comes to the sauna, it's the Scandinavians who know best. There's many a time the effects of a Stockholm all-nighter have been alleviated by a morning spent naked in the hot box. The idea being that the heat draws the toxins of the alcohol from your body.

You have to take a few precautions, however. Saunas, of course, draw even more fluid out of your body than the drinking session already has, so neck lots of water both before and after. Also, be warned: some medical experts believe alcohol and extreme heat can lead to irregular heartbeats and, in extreme cases, cardiac arrest, so don't stay in too long.

In Finland, a sauna often includes a spot of gentle slapping with twigs to encourage the skin pores to open up. This is followed by a quick roll in the snow to close the pores afterwards. There's no evidence that either activity will help combat your hangover, but, hey, it will certainly take your mind off your headache. Especially if there are a group of naked Finns in the sauna with you.

# Coconut Water

+ several coconuts
+ a mallet

There's no complicated science behind this one. Again, it's a simple case of rehydration. Coconut water—extracted from the nut when it's still too young to form milk—contains pretty much the same electrolytes found in the human body. A mark of its efficacity is that it's occasionally been used in hospitals as an intravenous drip when conventional fluids have run out.

And, recently, it's become so popular that commercial drink manufacturers have jumped onto the bandwagon. One concoction, known as VitaCoco, has even managed to secure Madonna as an investor.

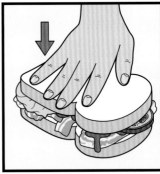

# The BLT

+ four rashers of back bacon
+ chunky bread
+ leaves of lettuce
+ a tomato
+ mayonnaise, ketchup, and butter

Sometimes comfort food is the only answer. And you don't get more comfortable than a bacon sandwich topped with fresh lettuce and a few slices of tomato.

Even the scientists agree this little beauty can help with hangovers. A study at a British university discovered that the protein in bacon replaces essential amino acids lost during binge drinking, while substances in the pork called amines top up the neurotransmitters depleted by the alcohol.

The other bonus is that a BLT is easy to prepare, even when you're stumbling about the kitchen in a post-alcohol fog. Start by grilling the bacon until it's crispy. Slap it between two pieces of buttered toast, add some crispy leaves of lettuce, a couple of slices of tomato, a squirt of ketchup, and lots of mayonnaise.

# Oxygen

+ a can of oxygen

If you've ever been on a skiing trip you'll know just how quickly your après-ski hangover evaporates once you hit that first run the following morning. That's all down to the oxygen in the fresh, mountain air.

Although it's not been scientifically proven, the theory is that extra oxygen speeds up your metabolism and helps your internal organs process the toxins from alcohol more quickly.

But most of us live down at sea level. We don't have the luxury of fresh, mountain air. Rush-hour fumes are about the best we can hope for during the morning after. So what's the answer? Buy pure oxygen in a can. Many companies now sell the product. You simply inhale.

## Liquid Legends

Was Genghis Khan a heavy drinker? You bet your herd of yaks he was. Nothing like a good booze-up after killing 40 million people. Although history doesn't show what his usual tipple was, it's highly likely this Mongolian favorite was his hangover cure: pickled sheep's eye and tomato juice. Some Mongolians still swear by it today.

# Cabbage Soup

+ two onions, sliced
+ one tablespoon butter
+ seven cups (1.7 liters) vegetable stock
+ half a head of cabbage
+ one can chopped tomatoes
+ one tablespoon cider vinegar
+ two carrots, chopped
+ one turnip, cubed
+ one potato, peeled and cubed
+ salt, pepper, and chopped parsley to season

Cabbage has been a hangover remedy as far back as ancient Greece. One of the by-products of alcohol are toxins called cogeners, and cabbage helps eradicate these naughty little fellows.

The best way to ingest the stuff the morning after the night before is in soup form. And you can't go wrong with the famous Russian cabbage soup. The Russians have always been inventive when it comes to cabbages. Not surprising, really, when you think how many long winters they've had to perfect their recipes.

Their anti-hangover soup is simple to prepare and will soothe both headaches and nausea. Fry the onions in the butter until tender. Add the stock, cabbage, tomatoes, and vinegar. Heat until it boils. Now reduce the heat and simmer uncovered for 30 minutes. Add the carrots, turnip, and potato and simmer for a further 15 minutes. Season with salt, pepper, and parsley. Be prepared for the ensuing monstrous flatulence.

# Guinness and Oysters

+ a pint of Guinness
+ half a dozen oysters

The Irish swear by it. (But then they swear by a lot of things. In fact, they swear whenever humanly possible.) The only problem is, if you're Irish and you have a hangover, it's highly likely you spent the previous evening consuming pints of the black stuff. This means it will take an iron constitution to bring yourself to put more inside your suffering body the morning after. Especially if you accompany it with oysters.

There is, however, some clever science behind the remedy. The Guinness acts in a hair-of-the-dog capacity, and also includes many essential nutrients. The oysters are believed to have a restorative effect thanks to their high levels of protein.

## Liquid Legends

Pliny the Elder was no fool. After all, it was this wise ancient Roman who penned the world's first encyclopedia. He was also a staunch advocate of raw owls' eggs as an effective hangover cure.

# Fernet

+ one measure of Fernet Branca
+ one measure of sweet vermouth
+ three measures of gin
+ one cocktail cherry

No one's quite sure of the exact ingredients in the liquor known as Fernet. It's all a bit of a myth. It definitely contains aloe, myrrh, chamomile, cardamom, and saffron. But, in Argentina—where it is normally mixed with cola and considered almost a national drink—there are rumors it also involves a bit of wormwood, coca leaf, codeine, mushroom, gentian, quinine, ginseng, and St. John's wort. Depending on which doctors you talk to, it can treat cholera, baby colic, menstrual pain, stomach upsets, and, most importantly, hangovers.

The trouble is, it tastes like cheap mouthwash on its own. The best way to consume it is in a cocktail. Try this lovely little number, using the most renowned Fernet liquor, Fernet Branca. Simply mix the Fernet, vermouth, and gin with ice and strain into a cocktail glass. Add a cocktail cherry for a bit of token vitamin C.

# The Full Monty

+ bacon
+ sausages
+ eggs
+ tomatoes, halved
+ mushrooms, halved
+ bread and butter
+ baked beans
+ cup of tea with milk and sugar
+ black pudding (optional)

Other countries mock the British contribution to world cuisine. "Chips with everything," they say with a sneer. But there's one UK dish that silences every critic, and that's the full English breakfast, aka The Full Monty.

It may be a heart attack waiting to happen, but it delivers the perfect combination of protein, carbohydrate, and fat (plus the cysteine in the eggs) that every hangover victim needs. There's even a dose of Vitamin C in the form of the fried tomato.

Preparation is both easy and greasy. Grab the largest frying pan you can find, add a glug of vegetable oil, and fry all the ingredients together—except the baked beans, which you simply heat up in a separate pan. Serve with fried bread, buttered toast, and steaming cups of tea. If you're feeling adventurous you can even include black pudding. (That's congealed pig's blood served in a pig's intestine, in case you're asking. And they wonder where the bad food rep comes from.)

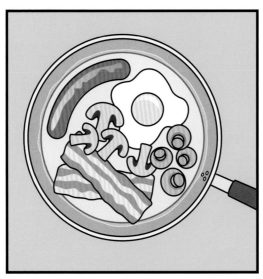

# Bloody Mary

+ five measures of tomato juice
+ a freshly squeezed lemon
+ a generous measure of vodka
+ Worcestershire sauce and Tabasco
+ celery salt and black pepper
+ a stick of celery and lots of ice

Who exactly was Bloody Mary? Some say the drink is named after the English Queen Mary. Others claim it was the Hollywood silent-film actress Mary Pickford. There are even suggestions it was a waitress in a Chicago bar called the Bucket of Blood.

Whoever the elusive Mary was, she has inspired one of the most famous hangover remedies of all time. First invented in the 1920s and championed by the likes of Ernest Hemingway, this infamous cocktail has soothed countless hangovers over the years. And it's pretty obvious how it works. The vodka acts as a hard-core hair of the dog, and the tomato juice injects some essential vitamin C.

Always prepare this drink with something of a flourish since it's really the only acceptable way to get drunk at breakfast. Fill up a highball glass with ice cubes, pour in the tomato juice, squeeze in the lemon juice, and then top it up with vodka. Add a dash of Worcestershire sauce and Tabasco to taste, plus a pinch of celery salt and black pepper, before stirring and garnishing with a celery stick. (For a Virgin Mary, follow the same recipe, but leave out the vodka. And shame on you!)

# Reflexology

+ easily removable socks

With all hangovers, it's your stomach and your head that need the most attention. Reflexology—which involves applying pressure to key energy points on the body—offers two quick cures for these aching areas.

Start with the head. Using the thumb and forefinger of one hand, pinch the tender spot between the base knuckles of the forefinger and thumb on your opposite hand. Take deep breaths and hold for 30-second intervals until your headache subsides.

Now for the stomach. Apply pressure with one finger to the second toe of each foot. You're looking for the stomach meridian point—the energy highway that leads directly to your stomach. It's the point just at the tip of the toe nail of the second toe, slightly toward your big toe. Use your finger to push down on this meridian spot with a circular motion. Do this for two minutes in a clockwise direction, then two minutes counter-clockwise.

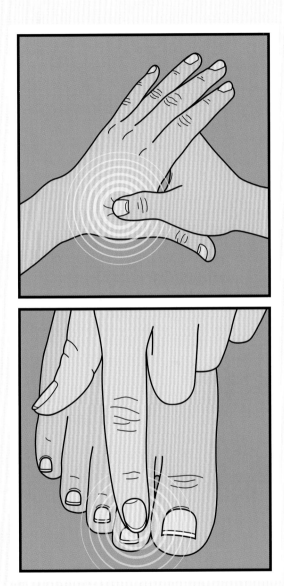

# Aromatherapy

+ peppermint, lemon, fennel, and juniper essential oils
+ a hot bath

Wake up the morning after a big session on the booze and there will be one overriding aroma in your nose. That's the delightful stink of alcohol seeping through your pores.

This smell obviously isn't therapeutic in the slightest. For aromatherapy, what you need are some essential oils. Since aromatherapy is not an exact science, the jury is out on which essential oils you need specifically, but many experts agree that peppermint (which cures nausea and upset stomachs), lemon, fennel, and juniper (all of which help liver function) are good options to consider.

To cure your hangover, run a hot bath, add a few drops of the essential oils into the water, and give yourself a long, relaxing soak. Breathe deeply to inhale the vapors into your lungs.

# Prairie Oyster

+ one egg
+ Worcestershire sauce and Tabasco
+ salt and pepper

Eggs and pepper sauce have been comforting penitent drinkers for centuries. A substance in the eggs called cysteine mops up many of alcohol's toxins.

One of the best versions of this classic recipe is the prairie oyster. Break a fresh egg into a glass—keeping the yolk whole—and add a splash of Worcestershire sauce and Tabasco, plus a sprinkling of salt and pepper. Hold your breath and down it in one. As you feel it slide down your neck, you'll soon realise why it's called an oyster.

P.G. Wodehouse's famous butler Jeeves was a big fan of raw eggs and hot sauce after a rough night. In fact, the morning they first ever met, Jeeves' initial service to his new master was to mix him up a variant of the prairie oyster.

However, the original prairie oyster—favored by cowboys on the prairies of North America— featured very different ingredients indeed. Instead of the raw egg, they opted for fried bull's testicles.

Here's a bit of free advice: stick with the egg version.

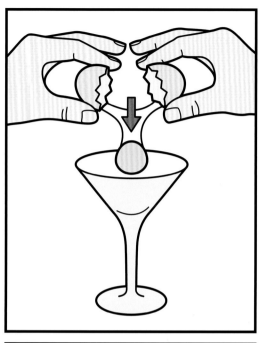

# Ginger Tea

+ fresh ginger root
+ water
+ honey and lemon juice

You'll know if you've ever had it. That mother of all hangovers where you feel so sick that you're reluctant to put anything back into your body, even fresh air. This is when you need ginger tea. It's been scientifically proven to cure nausea.

Be sure to make the tea fresh. Peel and slice up a small section of ginger root. Add the slices to boiling water and simmer for 15 minutes. Strain into a mug, adding honey and fresh lemon juice to taste.

In the Democratic Republic of the Congo, ginger is mixed with the sap of the mango tree to make something called tangawisi juice. They say it cures hangovers… and pretty much everything else you could imagine.

# Brisk Bike Ride (or Sex)

+ a bicycle, sexual partner, or both

Wake up after drinking your body weight in booze and the last thing you feel like doing is jogging round the park. But vigorous exercise will definitely help your hangover. It increases the circulation of blood around your body, encouraging your organs to process the alcohol toxins much faster.

Just make sure you choose an activity where you don't shake things up too much. Cycling is a good one since you're essentially sitting down, yet you can still get your heart and lungs working hard. And when you freewheel down the hills, the fresh air will give you an oxygen hit (see page 18).

What if your bike's got a flat tire, though? A gentle roll between the sheets with your other half might just do the trick. (Perhaps gentle is the wrong word, in reality the more vigorous the sex the better.) The exercise will not only help you physically, but also mentally (provided you are both in a fit state to put in a decent performance!), making your hangover a thing of the past.

## Liquid Legends

Chimney sweeps in Victorian London were notorious for their drinking. (So would you be if you spent your working day with your head up fireplaces.) Their classic cure for hangovers was a cup of warm milk with a teaspoon of soot mixed in. Apparently, the soot was used to draw toxins out of the body. Their other cure was to send small children up chimneys in their place the following day.

# Artichokes

+ globe artichoke extract pills

As far back as Roman times, heavy drinkers (and, funnily enough, artichoke farmers) have constantly been championing the globe artichoke as a hangover cure. However, modern scientific research suggests it might all be quackery.

Nevertheless, the plant does have positive effects on liver function, which speeds up the removal of alcohol toxins from the body. It also helps to calm nausea.

But before you start munching your way through raw artichokes, it's worth noting that you'd need to consume dozens to get any benefit. A much better option is to buy one of the over-the-counter globe artichoke extracts available in pharmacies, saving you both time, money, and the headache of where to get hold of 50 artichokes in preparation for the morning after a night on the booze.

# Yoga

+ a yoga mat

Both spiritually and physically relaxing, yoga is the type of exercise you can achieve even when you're sick as a dog. The yoga move perhaps best for hangover victims is a seated twist, which works on the organs in your lower abdomen. The theory is that the twisting motion helps your liver process the alcohol toxins.

Sit down on the floor with your legs stretched out in front of you. Pull your left leg toward your chest and cross it over your right thigh. Breathe in, sit up tall, and then twist your torso round to the left as you breathe out. Then round to the right. Now swap legs so that your right leg is crossed over your left thigh.

Be warned, though. Yoga sends energy around the body and relaxes your muscles (yes, all of them), so it often causes flatulence. If you've been on the beer the night before, you may want to practice your twists in the privacy of your own home. Farting in front of strangers is never a good move.

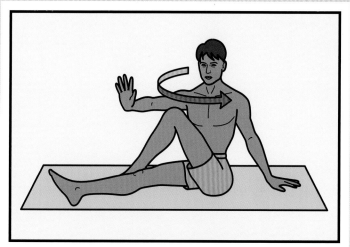

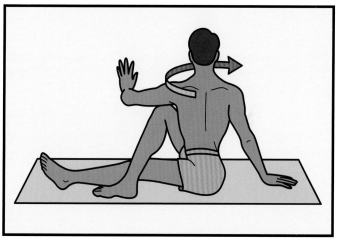

# Elvis Sandwich

+ one ripe banana
+ two slices of white bread
+ two tablespoons of smooth peanut butter
+ two tablespoons of butter
+ two rashers of bacon (optional)

No one gobbled up the peanut butter and banana sandwiches quite like The King. Which is why this hangover-numbing sandwich will always be known as the Elvis.

Like all the best remedies, it's easy to prepare. Mash the banana, toast the bread, and grace one slice with the peanut butter, the other with the mashed banana. Once you've connected both sides of the sandwich, fry your creation in the butter until both sides are golden brown. If you are feeling particularly rough, try adding one of Elvis' favorite ingredients to the mix: bacon. Apparently that's how his mother used to make them for him.

Before you stuff your face, pop on a white leather rhinestone suit and call your heart surgeon.

# French Child's Breakfast

+ croissants
+ one jar of chocolate spread
+ one mug of milk
+ cocoa powder (check packet for amount needed to make one mug)
+ a view of the Eiffel Tower from your kitchen window

Walk into any family home, anywhere in France, at 8am, and chances are your nostrils will be filled with the gorgeous smell of freshly baked croissants, steaming hot chocolate, and Nutella chocolate spread.

From a very early age, French kids are encouraged to overdose on chocolate at breakfast time. Perhaps it's because their parents know they face a lifelong love affair with wine. Whatever the reason, there's no doubting the restorative effects of the full-butter croissants and *beaucoup de chocolat*.

Heat the croissants for a few minutes in the oven. Heat up the milk in a saucepan (the French use UHT milk), and add it to the cocoa powder, mixing vigorously. When the croissants are warm, remove them from the oven and smear them with chocolate spread. Nutella is the Frenchies' favorite.

## Liquid Legends

The worst hangover in history? That award may well go to a 37-year-old Scotsman who went to hospital after suffering four weeks of non-stop headaches and blurry vision. It turned out he'd been on a four-day binge session during which he'd necked over 60 pints of beer.

# Banana Split

+ two bananas
+ vanilla, chocolate, and strawberry ice cream
+ chocolate, toffee, and strawberry sauce
+ crushed mixed nuts
+ whipped cream
+ glacé cherries
+ wafers

Too much booze seriously depletes the body of potassium and magnesium, both of which occur in bananas in decent quantities.

And the best way to wolf down bananas? The banana split, of course. Slice two bananas lengthwise down the middle and plop them on a plate leaving a small gap between them. Apply liberal scoops of vanilla, chocolate, and strawberry ice cream between the bananas. Douse the ice cream with chocolate, toffee, and strawberry sauce. Finally, garnish the lot with crushed nuts, whipped cream, and glacé cherries, then finish by stabbing the dessert with the wafers.

So easy, even a monkey could make it. Although he may struggle with crushing his nuts.

# Milk Thistle Extract

**+ milk thistle extract**

This Mediterranean and Middle Eastern plant contains a substance known as silymarin. There's nothing silly about it—especially if you've been drinking heavily—since it greatly improves liver function and helps rid the body of alcohol's toxins.

The best way to take it on board is as milk thistle extract, a tablet, capsule, or liquid available from countless online pharmacies. Ideally, you should consume it before, during, and after your drinking session. But let's be realistic, you're hardly going to head to the bar with a bottle of the stuff in your pocket. Try it the morning after instead.

### Liquid Legends

Painkillers were hard to find in the Wild West. You couldn't exactly pop to the nearest pharmacist. For cowboys, suffering after a long night at the local saloon sipping moonshine and playing poker, the answer was the dried droppings of jackrabbits, stirred into a cup of hot tea.

# Meditation

+ candles and a quiet room

The Buddhists aren't renowned for their binge-drinking habits. It's fair to say the Dalai Lama didn't get where he is today by spending his Saturday nights half cut on fermented yak's milk.

Nevertheless, many Buddhist chants have been known to alleviate the effects of even the worst hangover. This one, for example, which you should repeat seven times in a row, is supposed to cure your headache:

*"Om nama sri padma hum kar ana thaya hara ka pa la vyat ham."*

Should you choose to chant it on the train to work, however, you may get a few funny looks from fellow commuters. Much better to lie down in a quiet, candlelit room. Breathe in and out very deeply before you start the chant. In your mind's eye you should visualize your heart pumping nice, clean blood around your body, and your liver working efficiently to cleanse you of toxins.

# Atholl Brose

+ two parts Scotch
+ one part heavy (double) cream
+ one teaspoon of clear honey
+ ice cubes
+ one kilt and a pair of underpants (optional)

According to legend, this hair-of-the-dog cocktail is named after the 1st Earl of Atholl, a rather crafty Scottish nobleman who quashed a Highland rebellion by spiking the rebel leader's water well with his special concoction. Originally, the recipe called for oatmeal brose: water that has been soaked overnight in oatmeal and then strained through a muslin cloth. Since that requires a certain amount of forethought (which is always in short supply on boozy nights), it's a lot simpler to leave it out.

To make the easy version, mix all the liquid ingredients in a cocktail shaker with lots of ice. Shake vigorously to ensure the honey gets infused. Strain into a glass and knock it back. Preferably while wearing a kilt.

It works so well because the Scotch delivers you a hair-of-the-dog buzz, the cream takes the bite out of the Scotch, and the honey tops up your depleted sugar levels.

## Liquid Legends

Nothing like a bit of Haitian Voodoo to rid yourself of a hangover. In the Caribbean, it's not unknown for drinkers to search desperately for the cork from the bottle of liquor that got them into trouble the night before. They then stick 13 black-headed pins into it. Works every time.

# Bull's Penis Soup

**+** one very angry bull

The Bolivians like to cure hangovers and increase libido in one fell swoop. Their answer? *Caldo de cardan*, or bull's penis soup, which, they say, after a night of heavy boozing, perks you up in more ways than one.

And it's not some rare, high-priced delicacy. Wander round the restaurants of any Bolivian city on a Saturday morning and you'll spot loads of locals slurping the stuff. As well as the bull's genitalia, the soup also contains beef, chicken, lamb, boiled egg, rice, and potatoes.

It's obviously not for the faint-hearted. When you're nursing a headache and severe nausea, it's not always advisable to spoon a bull's most private parts into your mouth.

# Borage

+ ravioli or a bottle of Pimm's No. 1

There's some documented scientific proof behind
this one. In clinical trials, it was proved that *Borago
officinalis*, a herb commonly known as borage,
alleviates the worst effects of a hangover.

What wasn't scientifically proven was the best way to get the stuff
into your system. It looks like you have two choices, depending
on whether you fancy hair of the dog or not. You could either go
Italian and eat a plate of ravioli, which is traditionally stuffed
with borage. Or you could go British. They use borage to
garnish a gin-based cocktail mix called Pimm's.

## Liquid Legends
In some parts of Mexico, suffering señors and señoritas will lie in bed the morning after and pour a shot of tequila into their belly button. While they lie back and nurse their headache, the alcohol seeps slowly through the skin, into the bloodstream, hair-of-the-dog style.

# Smoothie Overload

+ 3½ oz (100g) of strawberries
+ 10½ oz (300g) of pineapple
+ one large banana
+ the juice of one lemon
+ ice

Too much booze gives your body a serious spanking in the vitamin and nutrient department. So it's not surprising your body cries out for healthy food the morning after.

Fruit smoothies are the perfect answer, giving you a major injection of goodness, with just a minor amount of preparation. Try this one out for size. It's packed with vitamin C, magnesium, and potassium, all of which will have been depleted overnight.

Peel and chop up the strawberries, pineapple, and banana before throwing them into a blender with the lemon juice and a handful of ice cubes. Blitz the mixture for around 30 seconds until you have a smooth liquid, then pour into a glass, and enjoy as the nutrients in the fruit work their magic.

# Eggnog

+ one medium free-range egg
+ a measure of brandy
+ a measure of dark rum
+ one tablespoon of gomme syrup
+ three measures of milk
+ fresh nutmeg
+ a Christmas tree

If Santa Claus were ever the victim of a vicious hangover, this would surely be his favorite cure. It is perfect for those rather fuzzy Christmas Day mornings. (Not that Santa would ever imbibe too much, of course. No, not with all that sleigh-riding he has to do.)

Preparation is reassuringly simple. Mix the egg, brandy, rum, and gomme syrup in a cocktail shaker. Shake it all up as vigorously as your hangover allows. Strain it into a glass before stirring in the milk and grating the nutmeg on top.

Now for the scientific bit. The cysteine in the egg cleans up many of alcohol's poisonous effects, while the brandy and rum obviously do the opposite: they take the sting out of the hangover by giving you a hair of the dog.

### Liquid Legends
Ancient Greeks and Romans may have been a civilised bunch, but when faced with a hangover they were forced to take desperate measures to cure their sore heads. In Rome they swore by deep-fried canaries and in Athens locals would sit down to a delicious breakfast of sheep's lungs. Definitely not the most appetizing of cures.

# Acknowledgments

Thanks to all my fellow drinkers who, over the years, have caused many a hangover. Especially Sally, Jez, Naytin, Lucy, Oli, Weeve, Dave, Muzzer, Adam, Dom, Tash, Chaz, and Caz.